WHAT I REMEMBER

Mary Marshall

at the age of 85 years

WHAT I REMEMBER

BY

MARY PALEY MARSHALL

With an Introduction
by

G. M. TREVELYAN

CAMBRIDGE
AT THE UNIVERSITY PRESS
1947

CAMBRIDGE
UNIVERSITY PRESS

University Printing House, Cambridge CB2 8BS, United Kingdom

Cambridge University Press is part of the University of Cambridge.

It furthers the University's mission by disseminating knowledge in the pursuit of education, learning and research at the highest international levels of excellence.

www.cambridge.org
Information on this title: www.cambridge.org/9781107505094

© Cambridge University Press 1947

First published 1947
First paperback edition 2015

A catalogue record for this publication is available from the British Library

ISBN 978-1-107-50509-4 Paperback

Contents

Plates

Introduction

By G. M. TREVELYAN

MARY PALEY MARSHALL was born 24 October 1850 and died 7 March 1944. A few years before the outbreak of the recent war, she showed me the draft of these memoirs. I urged her to say that they might be published after her death. At first she hesitated with characteristic modesty, and then took to the idea. After that she kept the typescript by her chair, down to the end, and amused herself from time to time by adding passages in writing as memory dictated. The University Press has now agreed to publish it, with a generous supply of illustrations which add to its value and realism. The editorial work has been done as a labour of love by her nephew, Mr C. W. Guillebaud. He had, only this year, persuaded Lord Keynes to write the Introduction, which now, alas, must be done by an inferior hand. But Keynes had written an excellent obituary of her in sixteen pages of the *Economic Journal* for June to September 1944, basing that miniature biography on this memoir now given to the public in full.

To Cambridge folk the book scarcely needs an introduction. It tells its own story in vivid and humorous pictures of scenes and people now long vanished: first we have a remote rural parish in the days of Victoria and Albert, as seen by a clever girl in the Vicarage, with a portrait of her evangelical father; then her intimate personal experiences of the very first beginnings of women's education in connection with Cambridge University, illuminated with a living portrait of Henry Sidgwick, all told in a manner worthy of the Brontës or George Eliot—(historically it is the most valuable part of the book); then Bristol; then a charming vignette of the Sicily of 1881 as seen from a flat roof in Palermo; then Jowett at his best Balliol period; then another Victorian type, 'the faithful Sarah'; and last the return to the Cambridge of the eighties, when the recent removal of the ban on married dons had drawn together a remarkable set of men and women. If people who knew not the Victorians will absent themselves from the felicity of generalising about them for a while, and read this short book, they can then return to the game refreshed and instructed.

Naturally there is a great deal of value about Alfred Marshall in these pages. I am permitted to quote what Maynard Keynes wrote in the *Economic Journal* (1944) about that great married couple, both of whom he knew so well and appreciated with his generous affection and piercing insight:

For the next forty years her life was wholly merged in his. This was not a partnership of the Webb kind, as it might have become if the temperaments on both sides had been entirely different. In spite of his early sympathies and what he was gaining all the time from his wife's discernment of mind, Marshall came increasingly to the conclusion that there was nothing useful to be made of women's intellects. When the great trial of strength came in 1896 over the proposal to grant women's degrees he abandoned the friends of a lifetime and took, whatever his wife might think or feel, the other side. But Mary Marshall had been brought up to know, and also to respect and accept what men of 'strict principles' were like. This was not the first time that her dolls (which she was in risk of making into idols) had been burnt by one whom she loved.

Yet it was an intellectual partnership just the same, based on profound dependence on the one side (he could not live a day without her), and, on the other, deep devotion and admiration, which was increased and not impaired by extreme discernment. Nothing escaped her clear, penetrating and truthful eye. She faced everything in order that he, sometimes, need not. By a gift of character and her bright mind and, I think one should add, a sort of natural artistry, of which I have never seen the like, she could charm away the petty or the irritating or the unnecessary with an equable, humorous loving-kindness. Neither in Alfred's lifetime nor afterwards did she ever ask, or expect, anything for herself. It was always in the forefront of her thought that she must not be a trouble to anyone.

Thus splendidly equipped, she now merged her life in his. Both at Bristol and at Oxford, where they were soon to go, she lectured on Economics, and when they returned to Cambridge she resumed her lectureship at Newnham, where she was in charge of the students for many years. She kept a watchful eye over the proofs and the index of the early editions of the *Principles*, and there are other ways of influencing the course and progress of a great book than open or direct criticism. The degree of D.Litt. of the University of Bristol was conferred on her. But she never, to the best of my recollection, discoursed on an economic topic with a visitor, or even took part in the everlasting economic talks of Balliol Croft. For the serious discussion she would leave the dining-room to the men, or the visitor would go upstairs to the study, and the most ignorant Miss could not have pretended less than she to academic attainment.

A good book might be written (and a bad book could be very easily written) on 'Great Widowhoods'. I have been privileged to witness several great widowhoods, of Mrs J. R. Green, Mrs Creighton and others. Among them Mrs Marshall's would hold a place. There is nothing in this memoir about that last period of her life. But for twenty years after Alfred's death in 1924 she lived on in their old home in Madingley Road, the delight of her many friends, the most picturesque figure of the Economic School, the founder and sure support of the Marshall Library of Economics which she made one of the great assets of the University. Again I am permitted to quote from Keynes' article:

First of all, his library passed to the University for the use of students *in statu pupillari*, to be amalgamated with the existing students' library, to become *The Marshall Library of Economics*. Next she set up a substantial endowment fund by payments under covenant, which she supplemented by paying into it an annual sum from the royalties of his books, the sale of which for some years after his death, so far from diminishing, increased. (In her will she has left the Library a further £10,000 and all her husband's copyrights.) But above all she decided to become herself in her proper person the tutelary goddess of the books and of the rising generation of students. So in her seventy-fifth year, defying the University Regulations, by which it is now thought proper that we should all be deemed to be deceased at sixty-five, she was appointed Honorary Assistant Librarian of the Marshall Library of Economics; and so she continued for nearly twenty years. Every morning till close on her ninetieth year, when, to her extreme dissatisfaction, her doctor prohibited her (partly at her friends' instigation, but more on account of the dangers of the Cambridge traffic even to the most able-bodied than to any failure of her physical powers), she bicycled the considerable distance from Madingley Road to the Library (which in 1935 was moved to the fine and ample building, formerly the Squire Law Library, adjoining the Geological Museum in Downing Street), wearing, as she always did, the sandals which were a legacy of her pre-Raphaelite period sixty years before. There she spent the morning in charge of the Library.

And so we saw her to the end, still in the front of work and thought and progress, but calm with a gentleness we usually associate with those who have long retired from life.

She realised the poet's blessing:

> an old age serene and bright,
> And lovely as a Lapland night,
> Shall lead thee to thy grave.

1946

I

Life in a Country Rectory, 1850–1870

THESE twenty years were spent in a rambling old house, its front covered with red and white roses and looking out on a lawn with forest trees as a background, and a garden with long herbaceous borders and green terraces. I did not realise the beauty of the place until I visited it years later, as an old woman.

The first thing I remember was standing on a table in the nursery in a red frock and being told that it was my birthday and that I was three years old. I can see that red frock still. Perhaps one recollects earliest the things that one cares for most, certainly I have always had a love for colour.

My next clear recollection is of flags laid out on the lawn, and of pasting large gilt letters on them to form the words 'Victoria' on the one and 'Napoleon' on the other. This must have been at the end of the Crimean War. While that lasted we were given a halfpenny a week instead of sugar in our tea, which was a good bargain for our parents as we disliked sugar in our tea ever after.

Of the Indian Mutiny what I chiefly remember is a diorama of some of its chief events which my brother and I made on a long strip of paper wound round two rollers and displayed in a wooden hut in the garden.

I also recollect a long passage in the rectory covered with life-size missionary scenes painted on calico, the one which I can best recall being the face of a savage chief with a knife thrust through his ear as an ornament.

Until I was ten years old there were three of us, my sister being two years older and my brother two years younger than myself. He was my great chum: we took long walks and climbed trees and collected birds' eggs (we only took one out of each nest), and I can still feel the thrill of discovering a fresh egg to add to our collection, and the terror of thrusting my bare arm into a sand martin's long, dark hole when there might be a peck from the bird at the end.

We were five miles from Stamford, the nearest town, and we had either to walk or to drive there in a pony carriage until as years went on a single-line railway was made to connect Peterborough and Stamford which had rather a curious history. The great man of the neighbourhood was the Marquis of Exeter of 'Burghley House near Stamford Town', and though the Great Northern Railway Company was anxious to run a line through Stamford it was forced to go through Peterborough and Essendine, as the Marquis would not let his own town be desecrated by a railway and for some years Stamford was left out in the cold and its trade went to Peterborough. As time went on the Marquis discovered that if Stamford were to recover its position he must connect it with the Great Northern, and at his own expense, by a line to Essendine, and my sister remembers seeing the Exeter coat of arms emblazoned on the carriages. However, the dilatory action of the Marquis, though it injured the trade of Stamford, helped to keep the place unspoilt. In later years when returning there I realised how beautiful it was and recollected how Sir Walter Scott always took off his hat to St Mary's Church which stood on the top of 'the finest street between Edinburgh and London'.

The Parish consisted of two small villages, a hamlet and two churches, all within a mile and with a population of little over two hundred. There were two schools, one of them being a Dame school kept by a Mrs Sopps, who was a washerwoman by profession and also a monthly nurse. She was supposed to teach reading, writing and summing. She certainly taught knitting to boys as well as girls and made active use of a birch rod tied with blue ribbon, both in church and school, bowing and curtseying to their betters being an important part of her system. There was a Sunday School in each village, and the children were catechised in church. If a child behaved badly in church it was shut up in a dark 'flour cupboard' in the rectory. If it told a lie in school a tongue of red cloth was fastened to its chin.

The Hall, a large mansion in a park and with a private avenue to the church, was occupied in turn by various odd families. The earliest I remember combined ostentation with economy. They drove about in a carriage and pair with coachman and footman in crimson plush smalls and white stockings. But once when I went there to tea with a boy friend a solitary strawberry was divided between us 'because it is so big', and the drawing-room had its furniture swathed in brown holland and was only used on grand occasions. At about that time I stayed with my grandparents near York, and was sometimes taken to see two old maiden ladies where I had to walk on the newspaper paths which were laid down to the chairs, but I don't think that this was done at the Hall. A later occupant of the Hall would on one Sunday ride about the village with her friends singing 'Champagne Charlie' and on the next would appear in church dressed in pale blue satin and jewels.

There were four or five farmers, uneducated and boorish, who were required to house a certain proportion of the hounds kept by the squire and there were one or two idiots who were kept for the most part in their homes and seldom wandered about. The villagers never failed to drop a curtsey or pull a lock of hair; they had large families and it was not uncommon for young couples to put off marriage till the birth of the first child was expected. Many of the children were named after Old Testament worthies such as Amos, Ezekiel, Obadiah, Keziah, and after a long search for a biblical name for a dog, it was called 'Moreover'.

Old ways prevailed in the church. In my time the clerk played a concertina which had recently taken the place of the village band. He read out the hymn line by line, sometimes with an introduction. The hymn with which he welcomed my mother when she came as a bride began: 'When Abraham his servant to procure a wife for Isaac sent,' which he told the congregation was 'suitable to the occasion'. He would put the two candles on the pulpit ledge with a warning: 'They be kicklish, sir.' A widow having died during the week he came to the reading desk and whispered aloud: 'Mrs Newman's compliments, sir, and she wishes to be buried on Tuesday.' There was no dissenting chapel and the church attendance was very small, but funerals caused much interest. The Rector stood in a movable shelter in bad weather and the coffin was followed by an old woman who carried a crowd of hats belonging to the pall bearers.

The village was fairly self-sufficing. There was a small general shop, a blacksmith, a shoemaker called Popple who made and mended our shoes, a bakery where the Sunday dinners were cooked, to which the villagers, who ought to have been at morning service, could be seen running with pies and puddings. There was also a carpenter, John Wiles, a clever carver. When the church was restored he did all the woodwork and the finials to the pews, and the pulpit and reading desk were carved in excellent taste.

I believe that after the Crimean War, as after the War of 1914–18, smoking became the fashion as officers introduced the habit on their return to England, but during the sixties and seventies it was considered ungentlemanly and my father fully shared this view. The only smokers I can remember were old women of the village with their short clay pipes.

Whilst we were children three servants were kept, cook, housemaid and nurse. The house was large and rambling. The coal had to be lugged up many steps from the cellar, all water was brought from the pump, and the floors of the kitchen and other large offices which were paved with stone were kept well scrubbed. Wages were very low. Our nice nurse girl was paid £5 a year, £10 to £12 would be cook's wages. Farmers' daughters came gladly at seven in the morning, gave a long day's work for a shilling and thought it good pay; and the servants generally stayed till they married. A man called Richard Hoggard did all the work of a large garden and looked after the horse and the pony. He now and then got drunk, once he was found harnessing the horse 'with its head where its tail should be' and when remonstrated with said, 'Some folks likes it one way and some the other'. His daughter was cook for many years, and said that she was 'saving up her wages for Master George'.

PLATE 1

ARCHDEACON WILLIAM PALEY (1743–1805)
Great-grandfather of Mary Paley Marshall

PLATE 2

REV. THOMAS PALEY
MRS JUDITH PALEY
(*née* WORMALD)

The father and mother of Mary Paley Marshall

Health was treated in rough-and-ready fashion. The village possessed one so-called midwife, a Mrs Lancolm, a very tall and stout woman who attended all cases, high and low. She certainly brought my sister into the world very successfully and probably myself.

Large pitch plasters were stuck upon our chests at the beginning of cold weather and remained there till the spring, when their removal was a painful process. Spring also was the time for brimstone and treacle; and cod-liver oil, castor oil and Gregory powders were used at all seasons.

Brass pans with long handles for heating beds were hung up as ornaments but they were never used, and hot-water bottles were an unheard-of luxury, though we suffered badly from chilblains. On the other hand, we were much overclothed. Winter and summer we wore flannel vest, calico chemise which reached to the knees, a much gathered flannel petticoat, stays and drawers with embroidered frills.

Our teeth and eyes were left to themselves. A dentist was never heard of. If a tooth had to be taken out it was done by Mr Higgins a chemist in Stamford. Spectacles were never used by the young and neither my father nor my mother, who both lived till over ninety, possessed a pair, though my father till the end of his life would read the newspaper regularly.

I cannot remember that we had many toys. There was a rocking-horse and a Noah's Ark which was kept for Sundays, Noah being dressed in a long brown dressing-gown. My sister and I were allowed dolls until one tragic day when our father burnt them as he said we were making them into idols and we never had any more. But we turned a corner of the garden into what we called our stable in which we kept some fine long sticks which were our horses. And we kept rabbits and hens and a Shetland pony called Jack who taught us not to mind being thrown off.

We had of course the usual children's complaints and got over them quickly and economically, for isolation was not thought of. We were all put into a room together and rather enjoyed whooping against one another and counting and comparing our measles and chicken-pox spots. Even diphtheria was not isolated and my elder brother died of it. I nursed my younger brother and a fortnight later had it far worse myself.

I can't remember much about our education till I was nine years old except that Mrs Markham's *History of England* was read aloud to us and Geography was learnt from two books *Near Home* and *Far Off*, and that we played scales on the piano. In 1859 a German governess came and more regular lessons began. History, it is true, was chiefly dates and we learnt them by a Memoria Technica, beginning 'Casibelud Boadorp', etc., and Geography was chiefly names of Towns and Rivers. But we were taught French and German pretty thoroughly and the family talked German at meals. Science we learnt from *The Child's Guide to Knowledge* and *Brewer's Guide*. All I now remember of these is the date at which black silk stockings came into England and 'What to do in a thunderstorm at night', the answer being: 'Draw your bed into the middle of the room, commend your soul to Almighty God and go to sleep.' We did a little Latin and even Hebrew with my father and some Euclid. As to story books, we read *The Wide Wide World*, *Holiday House*, *Henry and his Bearer*, and *Sandford and Merton*. On Sundays we learnt the church catechism, collects, hymns and Cowper's poems, there was a periodical called *Sunday at Home* and we read and re-read the *Pilgrim's Progress* and the *Fairchild Family*. This had a prayer and a hymn at the end of each chapter, and some children I knew took all the prayers and hymns at a gulp, so as to get them over and then freely enjoyed that entertaining book. But our chief knowledge of literature came in the evenings when my father read aloud to us. He took us through *The Arabian Nights*, *Gulliver's Travels*, the *Iliad* and *Odyssey*, translations of the Greek dramatists, Shakespeare's plays and, most beloved of all, Scott's novels. These we acted in the garden and called ourselves by our heroes' names. The evening hour was looked forward to all day long and its memory has followed me through life. One point about this reading has always puzzled me. Though Scott was approved Dickens was forbidden. I was grown up before I read *David Copperfield* and then it had to be in secret. I suppose that there is a religious tone in Scott which is absent in Dickens.

Very much was thought of 'Deportment' and my mother had a horror of what she called 'poking'. We repeated our lessons standing in a row with round wooden trenchers on our heads decorated with gilt paper which we called 'crowns' and I, being inclined to 'poke', had to lie flat on a reclining board whilst learning lessons.

Regular education stopped when I was about thirteen, and our Fräulein married the chief farmer in the village. During the following year my sister and I went once a week to a select school for young ladies in our nearest town, kept by two maiden ladies, where we were taught 'Mangnall's Questions', the 'use of the globes' and deportment. Our education was then 'finished' and for the next two or three years we read and did much as we chose. There were exciting events now and then. My mother took us to the 1862 Exhibition, a tiring business. We drove nine miles to Peterborough in the pony carriage, took a slow train to London, spent a few hours at the Exhibition, ate many ices and were very sick on the drive home. We also now and then spent a few days in London, and were sometimes driven away by bugs in the lodgings which in those days, before the introduction of iron bedsteads, were not uncommon. In the summer and as long as we were children life in the country rectory was pleasant enough. There were games in the garden, rounders and archery and croquet with comfortable wide hoops and a bell in the centre, and as those were crinoline days it was possible to move balls to convenient positions without being detected. Friends came to stay, not for a week-end but for at least a month. Every now and then we left home for a week or two. Hunstanton was a favourite resort. Of course we could not go farther by rail than to Lynn and then we took a donkey-cart or some other vehicle.

Later on, when we were growing up, we spent much time at Scarborough. We had a father who took part in work and play and who was interested in electricity and photography, and a mother who was full of initiative and always bright and amusing. We owed much to our excellent German governess. She not only taught us French and German and some drawing and music, but brought variety into life. She played games and taught us to act little plays and charades, was always cheerful and we missed her greatly when she married. It was after she left and when the governess stage was past and we had no regular occupation that we began to feel bored, especially in winter. The roads were muddy and had deep ruts (I heard lately that this word was no longer understood), and visiting the poor, practising the singing for the church services and teaching in the Sunday school were hardly adequate occupation. In fact an illness in the village was hailed with satisfaction as it gave one something to do. Now and then we might be asked to an evening party or a dance, but my father accompanied us and made a rule of carrying us off in the pony carriage at nine o'clock, just when the fun was beginning. Then the society of the neighbourhood was aristocratic and exclusive and much given to fox-hunting and horse-racing. My father on the contrary was a staunch Radical; if he met the hounds he would do his best to mislead them and if he attended the races it was to stand at the entrance and distribute tracts on the evil of betting.

He was a strict Evangelical, so strict that there were few if any of the neighbouring clergy with whom he could be intimate. Whilst an undergraduate at Cambridge he came under the influence of the Evangelical movement and his personal relations to Simeon gave a tone to the rest of his life. I remember the long row of the writings of Matthew Henry and Simeon which were gradually worked through during our somewhat lengthy morning prayers. He made little boundary line between the Established Church and others, and when travelling in Scotland he sometimes followed Simeon's example of preaching in Scotch Presbyterian churches. He was what is now called a Fundamentalist though he was interested in Science. An old friend, a geologist, who stayed with us threw doubts on the Bible account of the Flood and he was not asked to come again. He cared little for the outward forms of religion and had a horror of all tendencies towards laying stress on those rather than on its spirit. In his own church a curious screen and rood-loft which separated off the chancel were taken down and destroyed. A black bottle containing the Communion wine was placed on the table which was well removed from the east wall, and my sister was once rebuked because she pulled down the cloth so as to cover the legs, for 'the legs showed that it was a table and not an altar'. He always preached in his black gown and changed into it from his surplice in full view of the congregation. His sermons were unsuited to a village audience for they were theological rather than practical, and from time to time they were varied by a Homily from the Protestant Reformers Latimer and Ridley. But I have never heard the Prayers and Lessons more beautifully read, and in the words of one who had frequent opportunities of hearing him preach: 'To see the fine old man with his powerful face, white hair and black gown—earnest, stately and dignified—was like a leaf out of the history of the past.'[1]

[1] See Appendix.

II

Cambridge and the beginnings of Newnham, 1870–1875

WHEN I was eighteen my sister married, and as life in the country village became duller than ever I thought I had better follow her example. In those days women married earlier than now and the notion was common that if a girl did not marry or at any rate become engaged by twenty she was not likely to marry at all. So I became engaged. He was an officer and had to go off to India for three years almost at once. During his absence, as the Cambridge Higher Local Examination for women over eighteen came into being in 1869, I, for want of something to do, spent my time in preparing for it and when he returned we seemed to have few common interests and we broke off the engagement which my father had disliked and had never sanctioned. He and I had been working together at Divinity and Mathematics, I picked up French and German with our former governess and in 1870 and 1871 took the examination. The examination room was in London. Professor Liveing invigilated, and Miss Clough came and comforted me when I was floored by the paper on Conic Sections and was crying over it. She said that perhaps I had done better in other subjects. In fact I got distinction in Divinity and German, and so, in spite of the defect in Conic Sections, when my father and I were travelling in Skye that summer, the news came that a scholarship was offered on condition that I came up to·Cambridge to live with Miss Clough and attend the Lectures for Women which had recently been started there. My father was proud and pleased, and his admiration for Miss Clough overcame his objections to sending his daughter to Cambridge (in those days an outrageous proceeding); and in October 1871 he took me there. I was one of the five students who lived with Miss Clough in 74 Regent Street (now the Glengarry Hotel) and I well remember her white hair and large black eyes as she stood at the door to welcome us. My father and she became great friends and in later years when we had dances at Merton Hall I can see them leading off in Sir Roger de Coverley.

74 Regent Street had been taken for us by Mr Henry Sidgwick who had spent his Long Vacation time and money in getting it ready. In a letter which he wrote in 1871 he says:[1] 'I am not going to take any real holiday this Long, I have no money. The cares of a household being incumbent, I find myself estimating the expenses of Plate, Linen etc.' So of course we wanted to be economical as well and my first recollections of Mr Sidgwick and Mr Marshall are the evenings when we sat round and sewed the household linen in Miss Clough's sitting-room. This was my first sight of Mr Marshall. I then thought I had never seen such an attractive face with its delicate outline and brilliant eyes. We sat very silent and rather awed as we listened to them talking to Miss Clough on high subjects. But not always on those, for Mr Sidgwick was the most delightful conversationalist on any subject. I have known only one to equal him, Henry Smith of Oxford. Every subject Mr Sidgwick touched upon was never the same again. As someone said of him: 'If you so much as mentioned a duster in his presence he would glorify it on the spot.' His conversation made him sometimes inattentive to ordinary affairs and one day when he was helping us at dinner after using a tablespoon for the soup he pulled out the entire contents of the apple pie with the soup ladle, to our great delight. Though we were only five he found us rather troublesome. In another letter he writes: 'There is such a strong impulse towards liberty among the young women attracted by the movement that they will not submit to maternal government.' Perhaps in those days Miss Clough was rather inclined to treat us like school girls and in the small house we were at close quarters and of course had our meals together with her. But she was a woman, with great power of growth and adaptation, and from being

[1] This and the following quotations are from his biography by Mrs Sidgwick and Mr Arthur Sidgwick.

the mistress of a school in the North she gradually developed into the ideal Head of a College. Mary Kennedy and I were the worst offenders. For instance, one day we said to Miss Clough: 'We are going to spend the day at Ely and are not sure when we shall be back.' She did not say anything, but a rule appeared soon after in the *Report*: 'Students wishing to make expeditions in the neighbourhood must ask for permission from the Principal.' As it was we spent a happy day, chiefly in the Cathedral, and we ended by climbing the tower in the company of an agreeable young man but parted from him before returning to Cambridge. Mr Sidgwick, determined that the scheme he had so much at heart should not suffer from our troublesome conduct, came and gave us a good talking to and I as spokeswoman promised that we would turn over a new leaf. This turn was made easier because, with numbers increased to twelve, our next two years were spent at Merton Hall, with a dining-room large enough for separate tables, with its lovely garden where the nightingales kept us awake at nights and with its ancient School of Pythagoras supposed to be haunted, though the only ghosts which visited us were enormous spiders.

74 Regent Street could only house five or six students. Those who stand out in my memory were Ella Bulley (Mrs Armitage), very tall and majestic with a massive coronet of hair. We were rather in awe of her for she was the first research student and was allowed to read in the University Library, and was able to talk to Mr Sidgwick and Mr Marshall. Then there was Felicia Larner, the first of our band to take the Historical Tripos, and Edith Creak, a prodigy of sixteen, a great lover of examinations and who seemed to know Bradshaw by heart, and lastly there was my chum, Mary Kennedy, very beautiful with Irish eyes and a lovely colour. This caused Mr Sidgwick some anxiety. In after years Mrs Peile, a devoted friend, amused us by describing how in those early days of the movement he walked up and down her drawing-room wringing his hands and saying: 'If it were not for their unfortunate appearance.' Some of the Cambridge ladies did not approve of women students and kept an eye on our dress. Mr Sidgwick heard rumours that we wore

PLATE 3

MISS CLOUGH AND THE FIRST FIVE NEWNHAM STUDENTS
OCTOBER 1871

Standing (left to right): Mary Kennedy (aged 25), Mary Paley (aged 21)
Seated (left to right): Edith Creak (aged 16), Edith Migault (aged 16), Miss Clough,
Ella Bulley (aged 31)

PLATE 4

Above: THE FIRST HOME OF NEWNHAM COLLEGE, 74 REGENT STREET

(From a drawing by Mary Kennedy in the possession of the College)

Below: DIALOGUE BETWEEN BENTHAM AND AN ASCETIC

(Drawn by Mary Kennedy.) (See page 18)

'tied-back' dresses (then the fashion) and he asked Miss Clough what this meant. She consulted us as to what was to be done. Could we untie them?

Though four out of the first five students who were housed at 74 Regent Street in 1871 read for Triposes, during the next few years others who were not regular students joined us. I specially remember a Miss Tolmie, who inhabited what was called the 'nun's cell' in Merton Hall. She came from the Shetland Islands; she was quite six foot high, her red hair reached her knees, and she told our fortunes on All Hallowe'en. Later on she collected Hebridean folk songs from the Islanders, sang them into the gramophone and thus rescued many that would otherwise have been lost.

When I came to Cambridge it was not with the idea of reading for a Tripos. I wished for 'general cultivation' and chose Latin, History, Literature, and Logic, which last my father advised as being such a *safe* subject. He put me under the care of Professor Birks, a clergyman of strong evangelical views and Professor of Moral Philosophy; for one term I obediently went to his church (the quaint old St Giles with its floor sloping up the hill) and his Sunday 'At Homes', and taught at his Sunday school; but Mill's Inductive Logic and *Ecce Homo* and Herbert Spencer and the general tone of thought gradually undermined my old beliefs. I never talked on these subjects with my father but we both knew that the old harmony between us had melted away. In that first term I began to be interested in another subject. My chum Mary Kennedy insisted on my going with her to a Political Economy lecture. I resisted at first saying that it was only about wages and things which one knew all about, but she was firm and I went and went to stay. The lectures were given in the coach-house of Grove Lodge, lent by Mr Clay of the University Press for the Lectures to Women. I remember that lecture well. There were only five or six of us, Mary Kennedy, Ella Bulley, Felicia Larner being among the number. Mr Marshall stood by the blackboard, rather nervous, bending a quill pen which took flight from between his fingers, very earnest and with shining eyes.

In 1870 the only Triposes in existence besides the venerable Mathematical and Classical Triposes and the Law Tripos, were the Moral Sciences and the Natural Sciences which had started in 1851. 'This Natural Rot, this Moral Bosh', in the words of a Cambridge Poet, must have seemed a great innovation. In 1870 the Moral Sciences Tripos which had been leading a rather feeble existence for twenty years was the only one in which Economics found a place, and as it required neither Mathematics nor Classics it seemed suited for girls who had done little of either.

After the first year Mr Marshall encouraged me and Mary Kennedy to enter for this Tripos and we cheerfully agreed, though he said: 'Remember, so far you have been competing with cart-horses [Higher Local Examination], but for the Tripos it will be with race-horses.'

We had practically the same lectures as the men, but as mixed classes were improper the lecturers had to give their lectures twice over. Mr Sidgwick, who suffered from sleepless nights, sometimes dropped off for a minute or two and then resumed where he had left off. He once consulted Sir Andrew Clark, Mr Gladstone's eminent doctor, about this want of sleep and he recommended riding. 'Sidgwick asked whether running would not do as well. Sir Andrew smilingly consented and for years afterwards Mr Sidgwick took his exercise in the form of gentle running.' And he could often be seen running along the Backs, with his cloak flying in the wind. We began to attend Mr Sidgwick's lectures in our second year. They also were given in Mr Clay's rooms, and I remember Mr Sidgwick sitting to lecture with his back to a large low window. He used to frighten us by tipping his chair back and then just recovering in time. He liked to use his fingers when lecturing, he would make neat tapers out of bits of paper, and we used to lay out a variety of things for him to play with, red tape being a chief favourite.

He kept us in good order. One student cut a lecture. At the next lecture Mr Sidgwick said to her: 'You were not at last lecture'! 'No; I went to a tea party.' 'You should apologise.' 'Is it a case for two cups of coffee and pistols?' Before leaving, Mr Sidgwick said quietly: 'I shall expect a written apology.' And she had to send one.

Though the classes were not mixed, chaperons were necessary, and poor Miss Clough, having to do a good deal of this work, sometimes also went to sleep. At the end of a long economic argument she once woke up with 'Would you mind saying that over again Mr Marshall, it is so difficult', and he meekly obeyed.

We worked very hard, for we were pioneers and we had to do credit to the 'Cause'. We took long walks for there were no games. We were able, however, to go to the town gymnasium once a week with Mrs Fawcett as a chaperon, and she was the best climber of the long rope and could look out at the top window. Then Mrs Bateson, wife of the Master of St John's, gave dances from eight to ten in the Hall of the Lodge. She would watch the dancing surrounded by her four girls in white muslin and blue sashes (one of them, Mary, became later on a distinguished historian). There were undergraduates, who we rather looked down on as 'boys', and a few dons. Once, seeing that Mr Marshall seemed rather melancholy, I asked him to dance the Lancers. He looked surprised and said he didn't know how, but he consented and I guided him through its mazes, though being shocked at my own boldness I did not speak a word, and I don't think he did either. Sometimes our lecturers invited us to Sunday evening parties in their rooms, for five was quite a manageable number. When Mr Marshall asked us, Miss Clough took us first to the service in St John's Chapel and then we climbed up to his rooms—the highest in the New Court. On the first of these Sunday evenings, Mary Kennedy told Mr Marshall that he must not expect us to have our hair tidy as he had not provided a 'back glass'. He did not know what this was, but made inquiries and bought a very good one which I still use. We had tea and were offered crumpets and muffins which we consumed though with some misgivings on being told by our host that the first was 'slow poison' and the second 'sudden death'. A few suitable dons had been invited and after tea we looked at photographs which helped conversation. Mr Marshall had a large collection of portraits arranged in groups of Philosophers, Poets, Artists, etc. At one time he hoped to make generalisations about these groups so that by looking at a portrait one might be able to guess whether the face were that of a poet or a musician, etc. But later on he gave up the idea and was inclined to think that (say) Rubens was an artist rather by accident and could as well have been a great business man. The evening finished with a frugal supper of sandwiches and oranges.

In 1874 came the Tripos, which at that time was held in December, and till the very end we were not sure whether all the four examiners would consent to look over our papers. One was very obdurate, and when we tried persuasion we were scolded by Mr Sidgwick who said that we ought not to use 'personal influence'.

At the end of the second year Mary Kennedy had a severe illness, and Mr Sidgwick was most kind and sympathetic and a great help and comfort to Miss Clough. This illness prevented her from taking the Tripos along with me, but on the first day of her Tripos in the following year she told me that he came in his old green toga in pouring rain at eight in the morning because he had just remembered some little point which she ought to know. And before my Tripos he took an immense deal of trouble in coaching us and he gave us a short clear account of the history of philosophy which I think he made for us specially.

Though to my sorrow Mary Kennedy and I could not be examined together for the Tripos I had a companion in Amy Bulley who migrated from Girton after passing the Little-go; Newnham being more elastic as regarding examinations, she was able to extend her time of study by coming to us.

We were examined in the drawing-room of Dr Kennedy's house in Bateman Street, the Kennedy of the Latin Grammar. He was rather excitable and hot tempered (we called him the purple boy). He invigilated and sometimes went to sleep and we had to wake him up to light the gas. One morning he went off suddenly, to the horror of his rather severe daughter Miss Julia, saying he must go and get shaved.

But he made up for these shortcomings by concocting verses suitable to the occasion:

> No flattering tale it tells to Hope[1]
> That with their brothers girls can cope
> Bid the Superior sex defiance
> And take the palm in Moral Science.

[The Tripos papers came by 'runners', as we called them, who after getting them at the Senate House hurried to Bateman Street: among these runners were Sidgwick, Marshall, Sedley Taylor and Venn. At the Examiners' Meeting there was at that time no chairman to give a casting vote, and as two voted me first class and two second class I was left hanging as, Mr Sidgwick said, 'between heaven and hell' and Dr Kennedy made the following verses:

> Though two with glory would be cramming her
> And two with fainter praise be d—— her
> Her mental and her moral stamina
> Were certified by each examiner.
>
> Were they at sixes and at sevens
> Oh! Foxwell, Gardiner, Pearson, Jevons.

As we were the two first of Miss Clough's students who attempted a Tripos we were made much of. The Miss Kennedys gave us very delicate light lunches, and after it was over they took us to stay with them at Ely until the results were known for fear that the excitement might be too great for us.]

As to our books and lectures at that time, 1871–4. All our teaching had been done by weekly or fortnightly papers, without coaching or supervision. Mr Marshall was a great believer in papers. He set one every week, which formed the basis of his following week's lectures, and these papers, with the long red ink comments, were a great event. He set us now and then examination questions and used to say that the ideal examination question was one in which 'a lamb could wade and an

[1] Beresford Hope.

elephant could swim'. Our main teachers were Sidgwick and Marshall. There were indeed two Professors in Moral Sciences: Birks who succeeded F. W. Maurice as Professor of Moral Philosophy in competition with Mr Sidgwick, and Professor Fawcett who was then Postmaster-General, but we did not attend their lectures. We had a great veneration for Professor Fawcett. We heard how he was blinded when a young man, how he never saw his wife but was drawn to her by hearing her talk with enthusiasm of President Lincoln, and how he was determined that though blind, he would make his life a success. Sidgwick wrote of him: 'In spite of all that I have read of saints and sages I feel that if grievous physical calamity came upon me I would turn for strength to his example.'

The subjects for the Tripos were Logic, Political Economy, Mental, Moral and Political Philosophy. Logic was taught us by Mr Venn, the father of the present Dr Venn, and the text-book was Mill's *Logic*. He gave us delightfully clear and concise lectures on Mill's four methods and illustrated each from the cultivation of plants in his own garden. He was a wonderful gardener and could even grow Edelweiss. His son told me that when his father was at a Swiss table d'hôte and wore Edelweiss in his buttonhole, his neighbours asked him how he had managed to climb high enough to get such a fine specimen, and he said: 'It is from my garden in Cambridge.' As our Tripos drew near we took to riding and he went with us, and I remember him pointing to a dilapidated farm at the foot of the Gogs and saying that it always made him think of Ricardo's farm on the 'Margin of Cultivation'.

For Mental Science Bain was the text-book on which Mr Sidgwick lectured, and the lectures and those which he gave on Political Philosophy were the basis of his *Elements of Politics*. Mr Marshall also gave a course on Moral and Political Philosophy scattered over the years 1873-4. This was chiefly on Bentham and Mill's Utilitarianism, and one of the papers set was a 'Dialogue between Bentham and an Ascetic' which Mary Kennedy headed with a clever sketch of the two seated in a railway station and discussing. In answer to this question Mr Marshall said:

PLATE 5

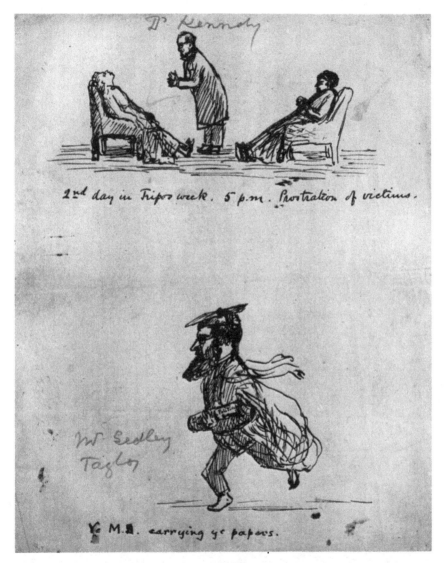

TRIPOS WEEK

(Drawn by Amy Bulley.) (See page 17)

PLATE 6

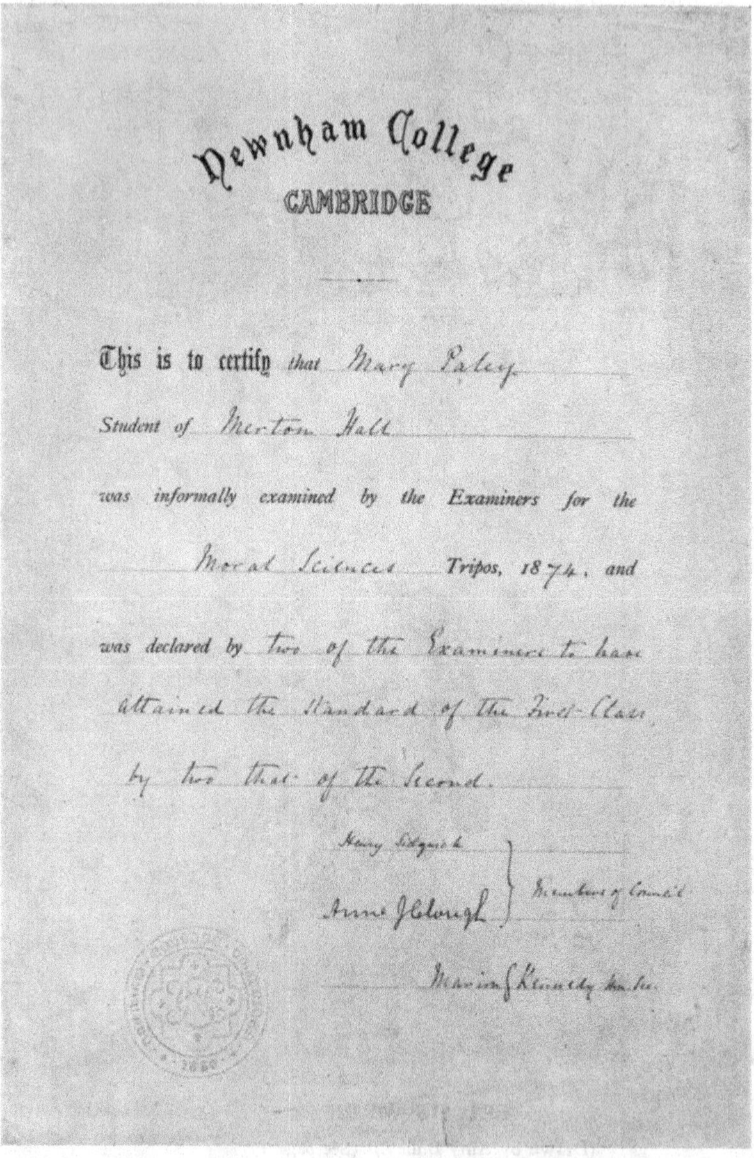

Newnham College
CAMBRIDGE

This is to certify that *Mary Paley*

Student of *Merton Hall*

was informally examined by the Examiners for the

Moral Sciences Tripos, 18*74*, and

was declared by *two of the Examiners to have*

attained the Standard of the First-Class

by two that of the Second.

Henry Sidgwick
Anne J Clough } *Members of Council*
Marion G Kennedy *Secretary*

THE EXAMINATION CERTIFICATE OF MARY PALEY

(See page 17)

'There is a popular usage of the word "utilitarian" in which utilitarian considerations are opposed to ethical or are at all events distinct from them. I have tried to show that this usage of the phrase "a utilitarian philosophy" is so utterly trivial and foolish that it is not worth while to discuss it. I have argued that not only is ethical well-being a portion of that well-being which any reasonable utilitarian system urges us to promote, but that it is much the most important element of that well-being.' He also said that Bentham had more influence on Economics than any other non-economist, his contribution being the stress laid on measurement. 'When you have found a means of measurement you have a ground for controversy, and so it is a means of progress.' Later on he lectured on Herbert Spencer's *Social Statics* and *First Principles*, and he introduced Kant and Butler's Sermons, and Thomas à Kempis and *The Mill on the Floss*, of which he spoke with great enthusiasm. (During those years George Eliot was at the height of her fame, and *Middlemarch* came out in thin five-shilling instalments.) [In these lectures he gave us his views on many practical problems, e.g. dancing, marriage, betting and smuggling.] He would say that 'Life means a deliberate choosing an aim and working to that aim, and people should regard the steady performance of their work as giving them the pleasure that they need and if excitement tends to deafen our ears to the more delicate tones then it is wrong. Relaxation has the opposite effect for it gives us greater power of appreciating delicate harmonies.'

As to marriage: 'The ideal of married life is often said to be that husband and wife should live for each other. If this means that they should live only for each other's gratification it seems to me intensely immoral. Man and wife should live, not for each other but with each other for some end.' He dreaded the future of betting and thought that it might be a more serious evil than drunkenness. He had a horror of smuggling. 'It is a crime of a very grave nature. It is as much worse than ordinary stealing as getting drunk in church is than getting drunk in the streets, for it is an offence against the religious feeling towards the state.' About the same time he gave six popular lectures to women, which attracted a large class, in which he said much about right and wrong expenditure, especially of time. He was a great preacher.

Economics was, however, the main subject on which he lectured to us. In those days books were few. There were no blue books or Economic magazines and very few text-books. Mill was the mainstay, with Adam Smith and Ricardo and Malthus in the background. Hearn's *Plutology* was thought well of for beginners. Later on we read Jevons' *Principles*, Cairnes' *Leading Principles* and Walker on *Wages*. Mixed up with the lectures on theory were some on the History of Economics, Hegel's Philosophy of History, and Economic History from 1350 onwards, on the lines of the Historical Appendices to the *Principles*. He would give half an hour to theory and half an hour to history. He was keenly interested in Economic History. In 1875 he compiled what he called his 'Red Book'. It was arranged so that if a pin were run through its many pages at any given year the pin-hole would show what was happening that year in Philosophy, Art, Science, Industry, Trade, etc.

After the Tripos I returned home for a few months and gave a short elementary course of lectures at Stamford. Perhaps as a result of this Mr Sidgwick asked me to take over Mr Marshall's lectures to women students and to come to the Old Hall at Newnham which, thanks to the strenuous efforts of Miss Clough, was opened in 1875 and held about twenty students. Among these early students were Katherine Bradley, 'the Newnham poetess' (better known along with her niece as Michael Field), Alice Gardner, Mary Martin (Mrs James Ward), Ellen Crofts (Mrs Francis Darwin), Miss Merrifield (Mrs Verrall) and Jane Harrison. As I was the only lecturer I saw a great deal of Miss Clough, we became firm and lasting friends and I learnt to appreciate her noble character. This was the Pre-Raphaelite period, and we papered our rooms with Morris, bought Burne Jones photographs and dressed accordingly. We played lawn-tennis and Jane Harrison designed the embroidery for our tennis dresses. Hers was of pomegranates and mine of virginia creeper and we sat together in the evenings and worked at them and talked. I had known her as a girl and even then she was called 'the cleverest woman in England'. Though in the end she read for the Classical Tripos she was nearly persuaded to read Moral Science by Mr Marshall, and she always afterwards called him 'the camel' for she said that she trembled at the sight of him as a horse does at the sight of a camel. She used to declare that she had brought about my engagement to him by stitching clean, white ruffles into my dress on that day.

During the first Michaelmas Term at Newnham Hall, as it was then called, Miss Balfour stayed there as a visitor and took part in all that went on. Later on she and Mr Sidgwick became engaged and as Mary Kennedy and I were devoted to Mr Sidgwick, who had done so much for us, we determined that nothing should prevent our being present at the wedding; so we stayed in a hotel near St James', Piccadilly, the night before and watched the ceremony and all the interesting people and Mrs Sidgwick walking down the aisle in her ivory-coloured wedding dress and shaking hands with her friends. But my father was horror-struck and sent off post haste my brother—a boy of fourteen—to chaperon us (though Mary Kennedy was twice his age and I was not only a lecturer but a Newnham chaperon). I was in disgrace at home for some time after this escapade, but we were always glad to have accomplished it.

About this time Mr Sidgwick gave three lectures on Poetry. He had heard that some of us were scoffers and he was determined to convert us. In ordinary conversation he stammered, but when reciting poetry or poetical prose there was no hesitation. I cannot recollect what poems he recited except a few of Mrs Browning's sonnets, but he concluded with the last scene between Maggie and Tom Tulliver which reduced some of us to tears and then probably he was satisfied.

After Miss Clough died Mrs Sidgwick became Principal of Newnham and she and Dr Sidgwick lived there, and he used to say how much he enjoyed seeing the students and watching the growth of the place, which was of course to a great extent his handiwork. Albert Dicey used to say that the two cleverest things Sidgwick did were to discover (1) Miss Clough, and (2) Mrs Sidgwick, and it was indeed the making of Newnham to have had these as its two first Principals.

III

Bristol, Ways and Means, 1877–1882

IN May of 1876 Alfred and I became engaged. Miss Clough pretended to be shocked but I believe she was really pleased and that at heart she was a matchmaker. When I returned to Newnham in October she gave us a sitting-room where we made the first outlines of the *Economics of Industry*, which Professor Stuart wanted as a textbook for the Extension Lectures and which with too light a heart I had undertaken to write. It was published in our joint names in 1879. Alfred insisted on this, though as time went on I realised that it had to be really his book, the latter half being almost entirely his and containing the germs of much that appeared later in the *Principles*. He never liked the little book for it offended against his belief that 'every dogma that is short and simple is false', and he said about it 'you can't afford to tell the truth for half-a-crown'.

In August of 1876 my father took a party of us to Switzerland and my brother, Alfred, and I went up Monte Rosa: my first and last attempt at mountaineering. Alfred had been an enthusiastic climber. As a rule he went without a guide and at times lost his way and spent the night out of doors, and he was the first to climb the Gross Glockner with only one guide. But he now decided to give up mountaineering.

On our return we began seriously to consider ways and means of providing an income. Alfred's Fellowship would have to be resigned, and as he had come up to Cambridge on money borrowed from his Uncle, he had saved but little; and I had £150 a year, which even in those cheap days would not suffice. One plan seriously discussed was that we should become Board-school teachers. Just at that time, however, the Principalship of University College, Bristol, was advertised, with a salary of £700 a year, and after much anxious consideration

Alfred decided to apply. When a difficult decision had to be made he used to write out on paper the pros and cons and give marks according to their relative importance. We were afraid that the administrative work at Bristol would too much interfere with his writing, and as things turned out it did. On the other hand he was wearing himself out with considering how to make an adequate living and in the end the pros outweighed the cons. So in July of 1877 we were married quietly in the village church, my mother giving me away and my father reading the service: and as he would not consent to cut out the obedience clause we contracted ourselves out of it.[1]

During the first year of our married life Alfred was very well. We took long walks and played tennis in the backyard and he was able to spend his mornings at the College and also to work at the *Economics of Industry*. We were invited out a good deal and I had much calling to do, being told that the folks at Clifton required a call at least once a term. But besides calling acquaintance we found many real friends. Among them were the Dean and Miss Elliott his daughter, the Percivals (and later the Wilsons), the Dakyns, Miss Alleyne, the Frys, the Peases, F. F. Tuckett, the mountaineer of the Dolomites, and Dr Beddoe. Some of these still remain and as true friends as ever. I was therefore pretty busy socially the first year, but we were both anxious that I should help in the work of the College, especially as it was the first to give women an equal share in education, and during the second year I was allowed to give the morning lectures in Economics to a class which consisted mainly of women and I was also tutor to the women students. Alfred, however, would not accept the whole salary whilst delegating part of the work and insisted on relinquishing £100 a year. He continued to give the evening lectures which were attended by business men, trade unionists and a few women; they were less academic than those at

[1] Alfred's father and mother and two sisters, and my brother and sister were the only visitors. I was married in white, but had no veil, and only jessamine in my hair, and I went away in a cambric dress and an old brown hat so as not to look like a bride. [Extract from MS. notes used by Mrs Marshall in writing her Autobiography.]

Cambridge; and were a mixture of hard reasoning and practical problems illuminated by interesting sidelights on all sorts of subjects. Later on Lady Jebb told me that she went to his lectures because they supplied 'such good after-dinner conversation'. And there were plenty of jokes mixed in. One member of the class, Herbert Grundy, could not take in a joke at once, but a loud guffaw used to be heard like thunder a minute or so later.

Alfred seemed fairly well until the spring of 1879. We spent that Easter vacation at Dartmouth and one morning we went to Paignton and walked by Berry Pomeroy Abbey to Totnes and then took the steamer back to Dartmouth, and as it was an intensely cold April I think he may have caught a chill. On getting home he consulted our good old friend Dr Beddoe who discovered that there was a stone in the kidney and who said that there must be no more long walks, no more games at tennis, and that complete rest offered the only chance of cure by allowing the stone to become incysted (at that time of course an operation was not thought of). This advice came as a great shock to one who delighted so in active exercise, but he followed doctor's orders rigidly. He was not allowed to smoke so he took to sewing and mending and he would sometimes darn with fourfold wool so that the holes became thicker than their surroundings. Later on he learned to knit stockings and they were the best I have ever had, for the heels were done with smaller needles and with double wool in order to strengthen them and the legs were perfectly shaped. Knitting was a great solace until it was forbidden by Sir Andrew Clark who feared that it might cause some nerve trouble. Alfred was very anxious that I should not suffer from want of exercise. Tennis was still to go on in the backyard, in which J. M. Wilson, then Head Master of Clifton College, often joined, and Alfred would watch the games and was full of fun at tea afterwards. But though he was always cheerful and made the best of a bad job, as soon as he knew that he must be an invalid for a length of time, he determined to give up his post as Principal. A period of complete rest seemed to be the only cure and rest was impossible for the Principal of a new College, for one important branch of its work was to arrange for lectures in the small manufacturing towns in the neighbourhood and this meant journeys. Then the College was very poor. When 'Knowledge is power' was being proposed as its motto someone suggested that 'College is Poor' would be more to the point. And begging for money was an irksome task. Bristol was a rich city but unlike the northern towns which had become rich suddenly and were unaccustomed to spending, Bristol had for many generations been the home of the well-to-do, who understood how to turn their wealth to pleasant account and so had less margin to spare for big gifts to education. To change the Principal in such early days was, however, such an evil that we stayed on till 1881. During this year William Ramsay was chosen to fill the chair of Chemistry which had been vacated by Professor Letts, and not long after Alfred said to me: 'I can now resign for my successor has been found.' Ramsay was exactly the right man, and he was physically strong enough to carry on the work of the College without neglecting his own study which was perhaps the most important one for Bristol at that time.

So, fond as we were of Bristol and our many friends there, it was a relief to go and take the much needed holiday and rest. We fixed on Palermo, for no particular reason except that it would be warm and that the water was good, but it proved a perfect success. Five months of absolute quiet on the roof of a small Italian hotel, in blazing sunshine, laid the foundations of a cure, which during the following year or two became complete. By February he was so much stronger that we managed to enjoy the journey home via Naples, Capri, Rome, Florence, Venice and the Bavarian Alps, and at the end of the year's holiday we returned to our house at Clifton.

It may be asked how we could afford such a holiday so I will say something about our money matters, the ups and downs of which in those early years did not much affect our happiness. At first I kept rather careful accounts but afterwards when we got the 'feel' of our expenditure this seemed no longer necessary. Alfred never wanted to trouble about money so, though we had a joint banking account, I drew the money for our everyday expenses and he seldom wrote a cheque. But he always took a great interest in prices, and as he had at one time been Steward of St John's College he knew more about housekeeping than I did. He had a fine eye for what was beautiful, especially in furniture, and whilst he lived in College he had gradually furnished his rooms with things from Jolley's who at that time, in the seventies, were breaking up Chippendale chairs for firewood. He knew they were good but as no one would buy he could not spare their house room.

We married, as I have said, as soon as Alfred was appointed Principal of University College, Bristol, at a salary of £700 a year; this, together with my £150 a year, was in those days of low prices quite a big income. We invested my capital in a house at Clifton which cost £1,200 and as we were expected to entertain we kept two servants and paid the elder, a farmer's daughter, £20, and the other, a labourer's daughter, £12. From time to time, especially after Council meetings, we gave dinner parties of about twelve, the greengrocer round the corner coming in to wait and the food being simple and inexpensive. During the five years of Principalship we managed to put by about £200 a year and every summer we took a two months' holiday. During the year abroad we managed to pay our expenses, which came almost exactly to £300, by letting the house furnished for £150, and using part of our savings. During the five months in Sicily we lived in a cheap Italian inn on the top floor, which led up to the flat roof. In Venice for a few lire a week we slept and had breakfast in a fine old palace on the Giudecca and took our other meals in a *trattoria*, paying a lire a head for them. We never felt pinched for money and during a month in Venice we went to the expense of a gondola and a gondolier at five lire a day because at that time walking was to be avoided. Soon after our year abroad we went to Oxford and our total income there consisted of £200 a year for the lectureship at Balliol, about £50 which I earned from correspondence classes in Political Economy and £150 from our capital, coming altogether to £400 a year. Of course that was a time of low prices and we seemed to have as much as we wanted. We gave small dinners and spent the Long Vacation in the Channel Islands, leaving the house to be occupied by relations. When the Professorship at Cambridge of £700 a year came in 1885 we felt rolling in wealth and set to work at once to build Balliol Croft. We were also able to spend sometimes as much as £80 a year on books and to travel abroad during the Long Vacation. In 1908, as Alfred was getting a fair income from *The Principles* and as I inherited some money from my parents, he was able to resign the Professorship and have more time for his writing.

IV

On the roof at Palermo

WE were five months at Palermo, on a roof, and whenever I want something pleasant to think about I try to imagine myself on it. It was the roof of a small Italian hotel, the 'Oliva', flat of course and paved with coloured tiles, and upon it during the day Alfred occupied an American chair over which the cover of the travelling bath was rigged up as an awning, and there he wrote the early chapters of his *Principles*. One day he came down from the roof to tell me how he had just discovered the notion of 'elasticity of demand'.

From the roof we had a view of the *conca d' oro*, the golden shell of orange and lemon groves stretching a few miles inland, and of the mountains which met the sea on either side and formed a semicircle of varied shapes. One was so remarkable that it took the fancy of the old Byzantines. They treated it as a typical mountain and in various parts of Italy it can be seen reproduced in mosaics. Perhaps the reason was that its shape fitted it to be the resting place of the ark. During many of the clear autumn days Etna, 120 miles away, was seen peeping over a saddle of the nearer mountains, its snowy peak turning pink at sunset; and out at sea were the Lipari Islands some 70 miles off pale and clear floating on the horizon, and the sea was generally so calm that it reflected cloud shapes on its green and blue and purple surface. The mountains depended for their beauty on shape and colour for they were entirely without trees. They were formerly covered with woods which used to bind the soil and prevent its being carried away by the violent torrents which rush down the mountain sides during the rainy season. This sacrifice of its future well-being to the short-sighted gain of a few individuals is one of the chief reasons that Sicily, which was once the granary of Rome, is now so poor. When we arrived in October there

had been about eight months with hardly any rain, and the colour of
the mountains was chiefly grey and yellow, but early in November
came the first rains of winter and gradually the grey changed to green.

Though bright weather was the rule yet every now and then came a
disagreeable variety in the form of the sirocco: the wind from over the
Sahara which brings with it the red dust of the desert. At Palermo it
was dry for it had passed over Sicily, and it gave the mountains and the
sky an evil and a bilious look and it had most depressing effects on mind
and body. When you woke in the morning you could tell at once that
it had come, for you felt incapable of being anything but quarrelsome.
Life was a burden till it passed away. It not only made you disinclined
to move about but it had a peculiar effect on the mind; we found that
we could not even read a newspaper with understanding, a novel was
the most we were fit for. An Italian Professor told me that during a
sirocco he often lost the power of expressing himself and had to use
roundabout phrases. If, for instance, he wanted a chair he might have
to ask for 'the thing on which I sit'; so that at such times his lecture-
room was deserted. But the sirocco was a seldom and a transient evil,
constantly recurring joys were the sunsets with the blue-black mountains
standing out in sharp outline against the lemon-coloured sky, and
Pellegrino with his yellow cliffs blazing with colour and looking all the
more gorgeous because of the long purple shadows thrown by his great
outstretched limb. But in this tropical climate the hour just before
sunset has its dangers; a sudden change of temperature takes place and
such a heavy dew falls that newspapers and rugs become saturated, and
the chill combined with malarious vapours which seem to arise is apt
to lead to fever. I had a malarious fever during the latter part of our
stay which I fear must have been due to sunsets.

From the roof we looked down upon one of the little courts which
help to make up the charm of Palermo and which, together with the
habit of flats, prevent one from realising that it is a city of about 200,000
inhabitants. It was a small court but the most was made of it. The
trellis-work over the pathways was covered with vines loaded with

grapes, and there was a lemon tree and an orange tree and plenty of flowers. The houses around had their balconies paved with coloured tiles, which especially near Christmas time were inhabited by turkeys, whilst pigeons lived in holes and corners. Of course the absence of smoke, and the ever-present sunshine made possible there what would be impossible in our large towns, but the English back garden might take some hints from the Sicilian court. It is wonderful how a southern sky and sunshine can glorify everything. Like the golden background of the old mosaics it harmonises and makes beautiful bits of colour which under our grey sky would look mean and tawdry. In Sicily the yellow carts and the red handkerchiefs knotted on the people's heads and the pink plastered houses and the bright coloured tiles and even the coloured garments and rags hanging out across the streets to dry seemed all to add to the effect; and such brilliant light brings of course deep shadows, not grey but rich purple and blue, and the buildings are generally arranged so as to cast shadows.

There was a good deal of traffic on the Piazza Oliva and we could watch the Palermiton and the cart in which he spent most of his time. When we first arrived and saw a gay-looking cart, carved and brightly painted, we thought it could not be meant for real work, but nine-tenths of the carts were of this decorated kind. Yellow was the ground colour and the sides were painted with scenes from history or from the lives of saints. The mules and ponies that draw them were decorated to correspond, for with characteristic love of show the Sicilian seemed to lavish his little wealth in making his turn-out smart. But at the same time he treated his beast cruelly and fed him badly. The sticks and goads, the pace at which the animals were driven, the heavy weights they had to draw and their miserable condition were worse there than anywhere in Italy. It was wonderful how many people managed to pack themselves into these carts, but in Sicily everyone drives, rich and poor: no Sicilian walks if he can help it, and carriages of a sort were cheaper there than in any other Italian town. In Palermo the fare for a town drive was 60 centimes, in Naples 70, in Rome 80, in Florence 1 lira. On the

PLATE 7

MERTON HALL, SECOND HOME OF NEWNHAM COLLEGE
(1872–1874)

Miss Clough and a group of students with Mary Paley first seated figure on the
left of the middle row

PLATE 8

GROUP OF EARLY NEWNHAM STUDENTS AT MERTON HALL

Standing (left to right): Amy Bulley, Carrie Bulley, Felicia Larner, Edith Creak, Kate Vokins.
Seated (left to right): Isabelle Bolton, Lettie Martin, Isabella Orr, Minnie Hensley,
Helen Sullivan, Mary Paley, Emma Brooke

whole a drive in Naples was the cheapest, for the distances and hills there are great and the horses must be well fed to do the work, whilst in Palermo the roads were flat and half-fed animals could manage to get along, and the customers were chiefly natives. They, like their animals, seemed half-fed. In Italy and Sicily a poor man is never stout. We noticed the contrast between England and Italy. In England the working man probably on the average weighs more than the gentleman, in Italy and even in France the opposite must be true. The poor in Sicily seemed to be very poor, and if it were not for the climate their life would be most wretched.

So much for what we saw from our roof; but there were things which could not be seen from there. We had gone to Palermo for the winter with the intention of living in lodgings, but we soon found out that without being able to speak, not merely Italian, but Sicilian, such a thing could not be done. Lodgings in the English sense were not to be had, but only a flat; and then furniture had to be bought and a servant hired. The habit of living in flats was almost universal. It was a rare luxury to live in one's own house and it was quite as rare I believe to have a kitchen or a cook. Meals were sent up from a *trattoria* so that practically no cooking is done in the house. We got to know some ladies who could speak Sicilian and they managed to live in a flat very comfortably and cheaply. They had a Sicilian servant, but they never liked to leave the flat in her charge, they locked her in or locked her out. They believed her to be honest but a Sicilian cannot be trusted to keep out other people. Then they had to engage a market woman, for though their servant was middle-aged yet as she was unmarried she did not consider it proper to do any shopping: for there was a strong Saracenic feeling about women. In the streets one met very few, and women of the upper class were hardly to be seen at all, and never on foot; it was men who were walking about looking into shop windows and gossiping. The English were looked upon as peculiar and with special privileges, but still, an English lady, especially if she had pink cheeks, got more attention than was agreeable. I heard that in Palermo there were many men who had some money but not enough to marry on and were too lazy to work, who spent their time in loafing about making themselves agreeable or disagreeable to any woman they admired. The working classes were always most civil and had those good manners which come so naturally to even the poorest Italian. They were curious about a stranger; for instance, if I sat down to sketch, people would come running out of their shops to offer chairs, and on my declining them would sit down on the chairs themselves on each side and stay there perhaps an hour or two, for they seemed to have no sense of the value of time; but though sketching was made somewhat difficult they were only interested, never uncivil.

We had made an agreement with the padrone of our inn that we should pay him for our rooms and the necessaries of life and that we should buy our own comforts and luxuries. This was partly because we thought we should get them cheaper and better and partly because I wanted to do some shopping. The market was my favourite resort, for there one got all the quaintness of the place intensified, the colour and the noise. I always went there for fruit and as the price was ticketed one could not be much cheated. Grapes and pears were very good and cheap, but oranges and figs were disappointing; probably the best oranges were exported; the figs had sticks run through them and were formed into large mats, and some of the shops were entirely lined with such mats, which were very dirty, as were the raisons. In fact everything that could be dirty was so. If it were not for the absence of smoke and for the habit of using tiles instead of wood for flooring the houses would have been very dirty, and one seldom ventured to sit on chairs in the churches.

The localisation of industry was remarkable. If one wanted to buy photographs or an umbrella there was practically only one district where they were to be had and where several shops would be selling the same article. In the Corso there would be a group of glove shops, of boot shops, of watchmakers, of booksellers, etc., but chemists were an exception, as a law prevented them from settling within a certain number of yards of one another. One street would be given up to chair-making, another to brass manufacture and so forth. We were told that this localisation was to a great extent the result of gilds; and that formerly each trade had its own street and its own gild. Shops as a rule were very small, shopkeepers were inert and did not seem to care whether they pleased their customers or not. Capital was scarce, and work was badly done because good tools and machines could not be afforded. For instance, as good lenses were expensive it was scarcely possible to buy a large photograph in which the lines were not sloping from the perpendicular. Milk was very dear. We were told that this was due to the scarcity of pasture about Palermo, surrounded as it was by orange and lemon groves which were again surrounded by bleak hills, so that the only good pasture within several miles was a little grazing land on Pellegrino which let at an extravagant rent. But why did not milk come in from the country by an organised cart or train system? This would not pay because the mass of the people did not drink milk, oil was cheap and it sufficed instead of milk, and organisation would require energy, and energy in Palermo must be highly paid because there was so little to be had. And so the grassland on Pellegrino paid a high rent and milk was dear and it was chiefly the milk of goats which were fed on lemon rinds.

The two things that were first-rate were bread and water; not the sour French rolls supplied at the hotels, but the *pane forte* of the people, bread made of the flour used for macaroni. It is of firm yellow texture and a little goes a long way, but when cut into thin slices we thought it excellent. The water came from the mountains and was brought to the town by the Arab system of pillars built at intervals and connected by water-pipes.

Those were the days of brigands, so one was restricted to the town for walks. It was indeed possible to go to Monreale three miles off, for armed police were stationed all the way within shouting distance, but in every other direction there was a chance that one might be briganded and a piece of ear forwarded to friends with a message that more would follow unless a large ransom were paid. Whilst we were at Palermo Jane Harrison, who came there to study some metopes in the Museum, was staying at our hotel and she and I went for a lovely walk of about six miles round the base of Pellegrino. No harm happened to us, but on reaching home we found the whole hotel alarmed and we were soundly scolded for such foolhardy conduct.

After that I never walked out into the country but there was plenty to do in the town itself. The place I cared for most and in which I spent many hours, trying to make a picture, was the Cappella Palatina. It is small and dimly lighted by slit-like windows so that on entering from the sunlight hardly anything could be seen but a mass of dim golden shadows. Gradually, however, the wonderful beauty of outline and detail emerged. The outlines are Norman, and Saracenic workmen filled in the rich colour and oriental devices. Most beautiful of all was the golden apse, out of which loomed the great Christ's head.

V

Oxford, 1883–1884

IN October 1882, at the end of our year abroad, we returned to Bristol and continued to lecture on Economics for a year. In 1883 Arnold Toynbee, who had been lecturer to the Indian students at Oxford, died and Alfred was asked to take his place. He became much absorbed in Indian problems, but his lectures were not exclusively suited to Indian students, and as they attracted many who were preparing for 'Greats', which included a certain amount of Economics, he had bigger classes than either at Bristol or Cambridge.

At that time Henry George's *Progress and Poverty* roused much interest. Alfred gave three lectures on it at Bristol which Miss Elliott said reminded her of a boa constrictor which slobbers its victim before swallowing it. At Oxford he encountered Henry George in person, York Powell being in the chair and Max Müller on the platform. Shortly after another duel took place with Hyndman, who called forth Arthur Sidgwick's 'Devil take the Hyndman'. Bimetallism and Home Rule were also raging about that time and were subjects too dangerous to mention at a dinner party.

The Women's Colleges had recently started and I had the great good fortune of getting to know Miss Wordsworth, the first Head of Lady Margaret Hall. She was wise and witty, her *bons mots* were proverbial, and walks with her were a joy. Then Ruskin was at Oxford giving drawing lessons, lecturing to crowded audiences and inciting undergraduates to make roads. Toynbee Hall was being founded and the Barnetts often came to Balliol to stir up the young men to take an active part. The Charity Organisation Society had just started. Mr Phelps was Chairman and Mr Albert Dicey and Miss Eleanor Smith (accompanied by her dog) regularly attended its meetings. There was also a Society led by Mr Sidney Ball for the Discussion of Social Questions, so the four terms of our life at Oxford were full of interest and excitement.

These were the days of the 'Balliol rhymes' and we were fortunate in being able to know many of the originals, as Alfred had been made an honorary Fellow of Balliol College. T. H. Green, Arnold Toynbee and Henry Smith had indeed died just before we went there, but among Balliol Fellows were Evelyn Abbott, Lewis Nettleship, Andrew Bradley, Strachan Davidson, Albert Dicey and Alfred Milner; and life was made very pleasant by Jowett, 'The Master' as we always called him.

The first time Alfred saw him was on a week-end visit to Balliol in 1877, when the first Principal was being chosen for University College Bristol, Balliol and New having taken an active part in its foundation and government. During the visit Alfred and the Master talked on every variety of subject except the Bristol appointment, and on parting the Master said: 'I don't know what will happen about the appointment, but anyhow I am glad to have got to know you.' This was the beginning of a lasting friendship. My first sight of the Master was at a dinner party given by the Percivals at the Clifton College School House. He sat with Mrs Percival at one end of a long table, I as bride sat with Dr Percival at the other. I did not know who the little man with a pink face and white hair was, but after dinner Mrs Wollaston, noted for her sharp sayings, told me that it was the Master of Balliol, adding that he represented to her 'light without warmth'. He and Henry Smith were on the Council of the College, they came regularly three times a year to its meetings and generally stayed at our house, and these visits were a delight. They were such a well-fitting pair and seemed so happy together, for though Jowett was rather shy and silent unless with a congenial companion, he was quite at his ease with Henry Smith who was the most brilliant and humorous talker I have ever met. I used to sit up with them and Alfred till well after midnight. They might begin by discussing College affairs, but soon would reach wider subjects, and whatever they talked about was lit up by some humorous remark from Henry Smith. They insisted on leaving by an early train next morning to be in time for their College lectures, and as Alfred was not strong enough to get up early I had to pour out tea at a seven o'clock breakfast

PLATE 9

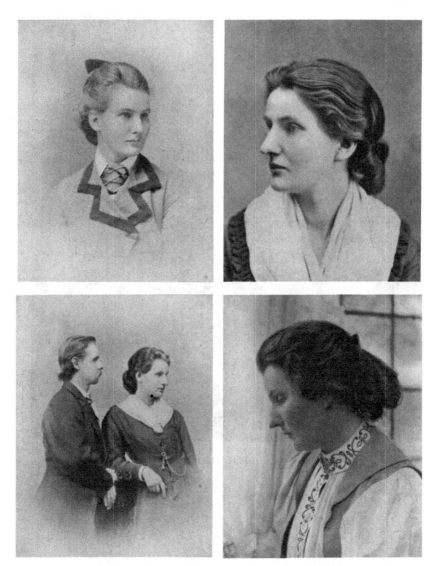

Above: Mary Paley as a student and as a don
Below: Alfred and Mary Marshall as a young married couple, and
Mrs Marshall in her early married life

PLATE 10

BALLIOL CROFT

and was very shy and silent; but they were so kind and gay even at that hour, that I was made happy too. It took me about five years to feel quite at ease with Jowett, for his shyness was a difficulty, but after a while we got on quite well and only talked when we wanted to. I sometimes took walks with him and he would make a remark now and then and fill up the gaps by humming little tunes. He always liked to talk about architecture. In later years he and I spent an afternoon at Ely Cathedral and he seemed to be absolutely happy there. 'I call this sublime', he exclaimed at the entrance to the southern transept. He had often stayed there and knew every detail. He made us describe any cathedrals we had visited, Chartres being a special favourite.

He enjoyed bringing his friends together, and almost every week-end during term he asked people to stay at the Lodge who he thought would like to meet one another or would be likely to help one another. His plan was to have a rather large and carefully arranged party on the Saturday which Arthur Sidgwick used to call a 'Noah's Ark' dinner, for so many strange animals walked in in pairs. One amusing pair was Lady Rosebery, a large lady, and the small Prince of Siam. There were the Goschens, the Huxleys, the Matthew Arnolds, Robert Browning, 'Damn Theology' Rogers, an Australian Prime Minister, Sir Robert Morier, Cornelia Sorabji and the Albert Greys among many others. I remember Albert Gray lying on the bank in the College garden and saying 'Aren't we swells to be staying with the V.C.?' After dinner a few select undergraduates were asked in and we had music. On the Sunday there was just the house party at dinner before the concert in Balliol Hall, and these small and intimate parties were the pleasantest. One of the most interesting conversations was with Sir Robert Morier as to 'the area within which one could lie'. And another was on the price of bread in which Mr Mundella took an active part. There were breakfasts too at the Lodge. Mr Asquith was at one of them and Alfred said that he had a mouth like a box, it shut so tight. The talk was chiefly on 'Fads', starting with vegetarianism, going on to anti-vaccination on which Mr Asquith had a good deal to say, especially about the people of

Leicester who had been giving him trouble. Alfred suggested the Referendum as a method of dealing with 'Fads'. The party reassembled at lunch when Mr Asquith was very interesting in legal gossip and in his description of Parnell of whom as legal adviser he saw a great deal. He said Parnell did not seem to like Ireland, and never cared to go there. A. J. Balfour stayed there for one week-end during the Home Rule period, and as the talk was chiefly on that subject Jowett said later: 'Of course what has been said goes no further.' Lady Airlie stayed there for the same week-end. She and Jowett and I sat and talked in the College Library, a favourite Sunday resort, and she told us about Barrie who was a near neighbour to 'the bonnie house of Airlie'. We had a good deal of fun and she made me laugh by saying to Jowett: 'Why, she's just a nice frivolous woman.' He then raised two questions: 'If you were not English, what nation would you be'? 'If you were not of the religion you are, what would you be?' and then described to us the religion of Bab the Persian in whom he was deeply interested.

He not only liked making his friends known to one another, but he liked talking about and sometimes criticising them and would sum up people in a sentence or two. He would say: 'Lord *X* is a pleasant fellow, but he has too much information.' 'Now tell me *Y's* faults, for people's faults are the most interesting things about them.' 'Only the most fastidious person could dislike Mrs *Z*.' 'Geniuses are almost always irritable,' etc.

He liked to spend a quiet evening with his friends. He came once to meet Albert Dicey and Eleanor Smith, the sister of Henry Smith, who was as well known for her brusque home-truths as he for his genial humour. Another time he brought Ruskin, who told funny stories and made us laugh with quaint rhymes about little pigs, and Miss Smith, who knew him well, said she had never seen him merrier. Alfred happened one day to meet Professor Vinogradoff and was so much fascinated that he asked him to dine with us and meet Jowett who had arranged to come that night. There was a little stiffness at first, as Jowett had not met Vinogradoff and as usual was shy with strangers, but as the evening went on talk became more and more free; after dinner we sat out in the little back garden under the birch tree and a full moon and then it became what Jowett called 'good', on philosophy and poetry. I never heard him talk as freely as he did that evening, and I would give much to be able to recall that conversation.

Being shy himself he naturally liked to be with those who could talk well. Once at a prize-giving in a girls' school he gave three pieces of advice: 'Learn to talk well, to read aloud well, and to write a good letter.' He enjoyed discussing economic questions with Alfred and would bring out his little notebook and take down a remark that specially interested him. He once told me that Alfred's talk was the best he knew. At another time he said: 'Alfred is the most disinterested man I have ever known.'

He tried to give chances not only to the rich and able but also to the poor. He discovered some talent in the son of his charwoman at Balliol, sent the lad to Cambridge at his own expense, and asked friends there to give him a good time, and he used to say that he liked to give young people pleasant things to remember. Like Mrs Sidgwick I believe a secret of his influence was that he always seemed to take for granted that one was acting from the best motives, which made one ashamed of acting from any other. 'Many a man by being thought better than himself has become better,' said the Master. Just before we left Oxford he came to wish us good-bye and he asked me to walk back to Balliol with him. He talked about old friends who had died and took me to his study where their portraits hung. He told me of one who might have been Dean of Westminster but who preferred to remain in a parish of East London where he had many friends among the poor.

Our faithful old servant 'Sarah' interested him and he was the only person to whom she would speak of her religious difficulties. When he stayed with us at Cambridge he would sit with her in the kitchen and talk them over.

Sarah came to us shortly after our marriage, went with us to Oxford and Cambridge, and died in Balliol Croft. She was a friend rather than a servant, and her fine strong character stands out in my memory. She was the daughter of a Somerset agricultural labourer, one of a family of thirteen whose father earned eleven shillings a week, and she used to tell of the shocking bread and rotten potatoes on which they were fed. Two of the thirteen died, but some of her sisters, whom I knew, were fine, strong women, able to walk their six miles or so when over eighty, and very capable, and during the forty-three years she lived with us she never spent a day in bed until a week before her death.

The year we went abroad she took service at high wages with an American doctor, and when we returned she wished to come back to us, but knowing that we could not at that time afford an expensive servant she insisted on doing all the work at reduced wages. She was deeply religious. Whilst Alfred was Principal we kept two servants, and her niece Lizzie, who belonged to the Salvation Army, was our house-parlourmaid, Sarah herself belonging to the Plymouth Brethren. When Lizzie had been with us a year she came in some distress to say that she must leave for 'Aunt Sarah looks after my soul so much that I can't stand it any longer'. I think Sarah felt a good deal of trouble as to *our* souls, but it only took the form of leaving suitable tracts about.

When we went to Oxford a schism arose among the Plymouth Brethren, not on account of doctrine but about the conduct of one of the members. The cleavage was so deep that those on one side would not worship with those on the other. Fortunately at Oxford Sarah had a good many companions, but when she came to Cambridge there were only one gentleman and his wife who sided with her and with whom she was able to worship, and after a while they left Cambridge and she was then forlorn. She was very unhappy, and when I urged her not to mind the schism as no matter of principle was involved she got angry and said she would go anywhere rather than worship with the Brethren, and finally she attended the services of the Primitive Methodists, though she never became a member.

As years went on she became an authority in all our concerns. She knew more about our relations than we did; she took great interest in the friends who stayed with us and they always remembered her. She became an excellent cook and loved having great responsibilities. Though she considered it wrong to 'enjoy' herself she used to say that the happiest week in her life was when the British Association met at Cambridge and when there were about twelve at each meal; she ran the whole concern and would lie awake at nights considering the menus for the next day. At one time she was troubled by the feeling that she was not being of enough use in the world, but was consoled when she realised that by good cooking she was keeping Alfred in health and was enabling him to write important books.

She made it possible for us to do what Alfred cared for very much, which was to ask poor people from Southwark, selected by the Women's Settlement, to stay at Balliol Croft when we left it in the summer. She welcomed and gave them a capital time and sometimes became a real friend. One of them, a delicate woman, told me how Sarah put her to sleep in the hammock and brought her tea when she woke. She said: 'It was like heaven.' She had her faults; towards the end of her life she became a bit of a tyrant and she had fits of gloomy silence. She nearly always gave notice in November, that most trying month, but I paid no attention for I knew she would not leave. One November she said she wanted to go to Australia, and as soon as full information about the passage, etc. was provided nothing more was heard on the subject. She spent little on herself. Our relations on both sides of the family left her substantial legacies, and she might have saved a good deal, but as she gave largely to her family and lent sums to so-called friends who never repaid her, she put by but little. Until the end nothing would induce her to make a will. She died in our house after a week's illness, towards the end of which she became unconscious, but as the doctor predicted, there were two short lucid intervals. One of these was used in getting her to sign a will in favour of her niece, Lizzie, who had come to nurse her, and to whom she had always intended to leave her savings; during the second Alfred came to see her (she was devoted to him), and after he left she said to me: 'He called me faithful Sarah, and what more could I want?'

VI

Return to Cambridge, 1885–1924

BY the end of four terms we had quite settled in at Oxford. The small house and garden in Woodstock Road suited us well. I taught the women students, Alfred enjoyed teaching his big classes, and though he always felt that Cambridge was his true home, we thought that our future would lie in Oxford. However, in 1884 Fawcett died and Alfred was elected in his place as Professor of Political Economy, the only serious competitor being Inglis Palgrave; and in January 1885 we went to Cambridge, hired a house in Chesterton Road for a year and in 1886 Balliol Croft was built and we settled down there for good. In 1885 prices were still low and the contract for the house was £900, though on account of a mistake on the part of the architect it cost £1,100. For several years it was the only house in the Madingley Road and we chose the site chiefly for its forest trees. Alfred took immense pains in planning the house and in economising space, especially in the kitchen department. He was anxious to have his study on a higher floor, as he thought that in Cambridge it was well to live as far from the ground as possible. However, J. J. Stevenson, the architect, persuaded him to be content with the first floor and a balcony. Later on, however, he preferred a large revolving summer-house, 'the ark', and devised a special method of wheels and cogs by which it could be easily turned from inside. He loved the grass and trees but cared little for flowers, and he took a special interest in the vegetable garden. He wrote to me once: 'I have always held that a kitchen garden at its best is more picturesque than a flower garden at its best. There is more depth and serenity and unconsciousness.'

One year passed much like another. In vacations, either at home or abroad, we spent some time in towns, seeing factories and workshops.

Alfred knew all about machines and tools, sometimes he took a hand in using them, and I have a jam-pot which he turned very neatly at Wedgwoods'. He could tell beforehand what wages were being paid for any kind of work and was seldom wrong by more than a few pence a week. One year we would go to the pottery district with its problems of localisation of industry and changing fashions. We were told of American demand for plates at four pounds each and noticed how the finest work was being done, not by the more delicate fingers of women but by the thick fingers of men. Another year it would be the light metal trades. That was in 1885. I remember specially the file-making industry of Sheffield where machinery was just beginning to displace manual labour, and we saw a girl cutting a file, who had only been at work at a machine for three hours, whilst file-cutting by hand required a seven years' apprenticeship. In the heavy metal industries we were told of the passion of the workers for the country, and how they would go for a twenty-mile walk on Sunday with their dogs and be fresh for work on Monday. One week-end we spent at Blackpool, ate potato pies at threepence each, watched the dancing on the pier, were struck by the good music and the fine faces at the Sunday concerts and noticed the Salvation Army collecting money for their brass band and saying that 'God ought to have a brass band as well as the devil'. We used to stand at the gates of factories when work stopped to watch the workers coming out. We frequented the markets, especially on Saturday evenings when the women were bargaining for their Sunday joints, we went to the people's theatres where virtue was always cheered and vice was hissed and to the Salvation Army meetings where the greatest interest was roused by those who could tell of the most sinful experiences.

In connection with a Social Discussion Society, which started soon after our return, we had interesting visitors, among them were Octavia Hill, Emma Cons and the beautiful Mary Clifford, one of the first women Guardians. At Bristol she used to be called 'the Guardian Angel of the Poor'. Then we had many working men to stay with us. I once took two to see King's Chapel where we sat for some time, and on my asking them what they would like to see next, one said: 'Don't show us anything more so that the impression may remain.' Ben Tillett, Tom Mann, and Burnett were among our visitors and a specially delightful one was Thomas Burt. He told us how he started working in a coal mine when he was ten and remained in it till he was twenty-seven, and though the family were all brought up in one big room he managed to collect and use books. He spoke of the great value of Mechanics Institutes, and said that on looking backwards the greatest change he noticed was that in his early days working men had no sense of humour. I believe it used to be said that 'Thomas Burt and Lord Iddesleigh (Sir Stafford Northcote) were the two greatest gentlemen in the House, and that it always filled when Thomas Burt spoke'.

In 1901 Mr George Trevelyan arranged a visit of the members of the Working Men's College to Cambridge, and one of them wrote an account in their Journal of a dinner to seven of them at Balliol Croft and of the three hours' conversation there. It sounds rather like that of the Walrus and the Carpenter, but it is so characteristic of such talks that I am tempted to quote it. 'We had the company of Professor and Mrs Marshall until eleven o'clock when the Professor took us back to our quarters. At his house we talked of the power of Niagara, of the tides, the sun's rays, of electricity and the accumulator Edison had promised us; of the best forms of houses, streets, chimneys and smoke consumers; of the beauties of the Yosemite, the Mirror Lake and the cause of its stillness and of its surface being ruffled at certain varying but foreknown hours every morning, of the giant pines there and the still greater trees of California. He showed us photographs—one of the Lake, in which so faithful was the reflection that you could not tell at first that he held it upside down—and pointed out the geological wonders of the country. Then we talked of labour and capital. He advised us in the Working Men's College to get someone to continue Ludlow and Lloyd Jones's *History of the Progress of the Working Classes, 1832-1867*. He was enthusiastic about Ludlow, and evidently valued his work highly. The names of Dent and Llewellyn Smith were mentioned;

PLATE 11

Above: Setting out for a morning's work in South Tirol
Below: Alfred Marshall in South Tirol (summer 1920)

PLATE 12

PORTRAIT OF MARY MARSHALL BY ROGER FRY

also Holyoake, but he was too old now and his knowledge of a special kind. A man was wanted whose knowledge was general of the conditions within the unions and without. He recalled having heard Maurice speak on the vexed question of signing the Thirty-nine Articles, which had to be signed at one time by all graduates at the universities. He told us that Maurice spoke against compelling men to sign them, saying that he believed them himself, and had too much respect for them to so besmirch them as to insist on their being signed by anyone who, though not really believing them, would so far swallow their scruples as to sign, in order that they might not be prevented from earning their livelihood. Then we talked of supremacy—English, German or American—of the causes of economic changes, of wars of our own, of the French and Germans and of the Americans, of our wealth produced during their troubles, of their advance since; of the relation between imports and exports, between production and importation and the sending abroad of securities and money; of the need for us to improve our methods and our education in things concerning the production of commodities, of phonographs, typewriters, hinge screws, nut and washer bolts, spokeshare irons, eyelet-hole punches, drug stores and many other things. No wonder, when we left the sweetbrier garden and passed out of the gate, that Harvey was so overcome that he disappeared in the darkness backwards into a dry ditch in such a manner that we could only see the soles of his boots. It was certainly the talk and the personal contact that we most enjoyed.'

During these years in Cambridge we had of course many visits from economists from the U.S.A., Germany, Italy, France and Holland. We were very fond of Professor Pierson and his wife, who stayed with us several times, and of Professor and Mrs Taussig. Professor Edgeworth was also a frequent visitor and kept us in touch with Oxford economics, and former pupils were always welcome.

I became a member of a Ladies' Dining Society of ten or twelve who dined at one another's houses once or twice a term, the husbands either dining at their Colleges or having a solitary meal in their studies. The hostess not only provided a good dinner (though champagne was not allowed) but also a suitable topic of conversation, should one be required, and she was allowed to introduce an outside lady at her dinner; but it was an exclusive society, for one black ball was enough to exclude a proposed new member. Its members were Mrs Creighton, Mrs Arthur Verrall, Mrs Arthur Lyttelton, Mrs Sidgwick, Mrs James Ward, Mrs Francis Darwin, Baroness von Hügel, Lady Horace Darwin, Lady George Darwin, Mrs Prothero and Lady Jebb. Mrs Creighton, who originated the society, had strong views against what she called 'sub-committees', conversation was to be kept general. And we had some good talks. When Professor Creighton became a bishop, first of Peterborough and then of London, the society dined at Peterborough and at Fulham, and if he had lived longer it might have dined at Lambeth. The society lasted for several years, but gradually some left Cambridge, some died, and the War of 1914–18 finally broke it up.

There seem to be fewer 'characters' now than in bygone days, but I had the good fortune to be on friendly terms with one noted character— Mrs Miller. Her husband was the Professor of Geology and her etchings of the Dolomite country (now in the Fitzwilliam) were so true that Professor Bonney said that one could learn the geology of the district from them (it was of course before the days of photography). She as well as I loved the Dolomites and she told me how she would sit sketching for seven hours on end absolutely happy and absorbed. She and I had both been brought up on Cowper's poems, and she could quote 'The Task' at any length. She had a sharp tongue and quick wits which much enlivened Cambridge society. I was told that at some dinners after soup and fish 'Mrs Miller's latest' would appear as an entrée on the menu cards. She was delightfully frank and amused me once by saying: 'Young married people in Cambridge often started in such small houses that one did not care to call and then later on built themselves such fine mansions that one was annoyed not to be on calling terms.'

Another lady who, though perhaps not a 'character', yet a marked feature in Cambridge society, was Lady Jebb. She came to England in the seventies as a young American widow, took the place by storm, and don after don fell before her. She used to insist on playing games after dinner, the favourite being 'Clumps'. In the end she married the shy and reserved Professor Richard Jebb. I remember seeing her at a dinner party given by Professor and Mrs Adams soon after the wedding and thinking her most beautiful with her lovely complexion and auburn hair. She was always full of life and fun and smart sayings. She would tell us how the other night when she drove home from a dinner with two Heads of Houses and expected to hear some high talk, they did nothing but discuss the sauces they had at dinner. She had also discovered that if the subject of *sex* was introduced at a dinner table everyone became interested at once. Once when the conversation was about servants she said that she believed very much in praise and ended by 'just you think how much praise is required by the Almighty'. On being asked whether she would rather be born beautiful or good, she said: 'Why beautiful of course. You can make yourself good but you can't make yourself beautiful.'

We spent most of the Long Vacations in South Tirol which we preferred to Switzerland. For in 1890–1912 the Dolomite region was unspoilt by tourists and motor-cars, and especially in the side-valleys the people were natural and homely and we made some warm friends; of these the chief was Filomena who kept the small wayside inn at Stern in Abtei Tal where we spent three summers. She was devoted to 'der liebe Herr', and when we wished her good-bye on our last visit she said: 'We shall meet in Heaven.' The hostess at another inn was very proud because one of her sons had become a priest and another the Professor of Ladinish at Vienna. He came home for the holidays and sat and drank and enjoyed life with his peasant friends, and once he brought an artist from Vienna who painted the walls of the Gastzimmer with Ladinish legends. One of them represented the mingling of the Latin and the Rhætian elements from which the Ladinish race sprang. The Rhætian woman agreed to marry the Latin man on condition that he should never touch her forehead, but as time went on he accidentally brushed away a fly which had settled there and she disappeared. In the side-valleys Ladinish was the usual language and many of the peasants could not speak either German or Italian.

One year we discovered that in the next village were assembled a large part of the 'Austrian school' of economists. The Von Wiesers, the Böhm Bawerks, the Zuckerkandls and several others. We boldly asked the whole company to a tea party in our enormous bedroom, which was the largest and most desirable room in the inn, and we afterwards adjourned to the tent shelter in the field nearby. Filomena was proud of having such distinguished guests and got up at 4 a.m. to make fresh butter and various delicacies for the entertainment. Von Böhm Bawerk was a wiry and agile little man, an ardent mountaineer who climbed a Dolomite almost every day. This somewhat exhausted his economic energies and he did not want to discuss the Theory of the Rate of Interest, a subject which I had rather dreaded, as he and Alfred had recently been corresponding warmly upon it. Professor Von Wieser was a noble-looking man and a delightful companion with a wife and daughter to match, and I much enjoyed the return tea party which the Austrian School gave at the beautiful old peasant's house where they were spending the summer.

Alfred always worked best in the open air, and especially in the high air. On rainy days he would sit on the balcony of the hay chalet and pleased Filomena by calling it her 'Sommerpalast'. On fine days he went into the woods where he had made a 'throne' with an air cushion and a camp stool which, when opened against a pile of stones, made a comfortable back to lean against; and there he would sit for hours absorbed in his writing. One day on looking up he saw a chamois standing only a few feet off. It barked and stamped and then went quietly on its way and next day it appeared again; and sometimes a cow would come from behind and breathe on his neck. He would choose the site of his 'throne' very carefully so that if possible there should be a fine view.

From 1913 to 1918 the summer had of course to be spent in England; in July 1919 *Industry and Trade* was finished and Alfred much needed a complete change and rest. His doctor said that if possible he must go to the mountains and he went to Folkestone to be in readiness to cross whilst I was to see after passports, etc. It was very hot, and I seemed to be sitting most of the day on the steps of Consuls' houses in a crowd. Then when we succeeded in getting inside I was told that I must return to Cambridge for references from bankers or others. It was quite hopeless, so in the late afternoon I went to Folkestone and we agreed that as difficulties might be even greater on the Continent we had better stay in England that summer. Probably the mountain air would have set him up as it had done so often; he began indeed to write his third volume but he was very jaded and in June 1920 we determined to make another attempt to go abroad.

When about 20 miles from Milan, at a small station, the carriage door was opened and we were told to descend as a lightning strike had begun, and that the heavy luggage was to remain in the van. With great difficulty we found a ramshackle carriage which took us and a suitcase to Milan. But when we got there no good hotel would admit us as they did not seem to like our broken-down carriage and insufficient luggage. After many vain attempts we were received by a third-class Italian hotel where we spent the next three days whilst awaiting the end of the strike. We could speak little Italian, and I don't know what would have happened but for Mr Churchill, the English Consul. He saw how important it was to get Alfred to the mountains and said that we must not wait for the luggage (he would see to that) but leave Milan as soon as the trains began to move. He also lent us his 'messenger' who spoke English and who was to see us off. On the third morning, when the trains began to move, we went with the messenger to the station who said, 'you take hold of my coat and let him take hold of you', and he pulled our suitcase and us along through the dense mass of people in the waiting hall where the air was full of bundles and belongings flying about. He succeeded in squeezing us into a first-class carriage full of people and we were carried to Verona. We reached our destination in the Abtei Tal without much further trouble, except that the names of the stations which had been changed from German to Italian were puzzling, and we lived on the contents of the suitcase together with a few purchases. I was haunted by the idea that we might never see our heavy luggage again for it contained all the MSS. relating to what afterwards became *Money, Credit and Commerce* though, curiously enough, Alfred did not worry about this; and how I did rejoice when in the midst of a thunderstorm six weeks later the luggage reached our inn in a cart, and thanks to the Consul it had never been opened or examined. This was our last visit to the Continent for with Alfred's loss of memory and increasing ill-health I felt that we must not venture again, though he always had a hankering after the beloved South Tirol.

The next three summers we spent in a lovely and lonely Dorset cove called Arish Mell, where he worked away at his third volume. But after *Industry and Trade* had been finished in 1919 his memory gradually became worse and soon after his doctor told me quietly that 'he will not be able to construct any more'. And it was so, though fortunately he did not know it. For in the old days he used to come down from his study and say: 'I have had such a happy time, there is no joy to be compared to constructive work.'

PLATE 13

WORKING AT THE MARSHALL LIBRARY (AGED 92)

APPENDIX

The Rev. Thomas Paley, B.D.

[Reprinted from the Eagle, *the Magazine of St John's College,
Cambridge, December* 1890]

THE REV. THOMAS PALEY, B.D., formerly Fellow of St John's College,
who died at Wimbledon on 8 August 1890 in his eighty-first year, was
a grandson of Archdeacon Paley, one of whose works is known to most
readers of the *Eagle*. He was born at Halifax on 11 May 1810, where
his father, Dr Robert Paley, practised as a physician. He went to school
there, then to Bishopton, near Ripon, where his father retired after
ceasing to practise, and later to Sedbergh: and he remained a devoted
son of Yorkshire to the end of his days. When young he was something
of an athlete; when more than eighty he could outwalk many men of
half his years.

He entered at St John's College, Cambridge, in 1829, and was a
scholar there; was 27th Wrangler in 1833, and elected Fellow 6 April
1835. His tutor at Cambridge was the late Dr John Hymers, of St John's
College. Tutor and pupil were much attached, and frequently spent
their vacations together in the English Lake District. It was during one
of these excursions that they made the acquaintance of the poet Wordsworth at his home at Rydal; a curious link with the past which Mr Paley
often recalled with pleasure.

Though brought up to be a doctor, he took Holy Orders, and for
several years held the perpetual curacy of Dishforth, near Ripon, where
he had pupils. The present incumbent of Dishforth supplies one or two
incidents of Mr Paley's life there. On a certain market day his pupils
took French leave and started off to Ripon. They soon discovered that
Mr Paley was after them, so they ran all the way to Ripon pursued by
their irate master, who chased them round the Market Cross and back
to Dishforth, cracking his whip at them as he ran. For those times he

seems to have had rather an advanced service at Dishforth Church; for he introduced stringed instruments, and every now and again there were grand choral services to which people came for miles round. Every Easter Sunday afternoon the children were catechised in church. Mr Paley would be in the pulpit—a three decker—while his sister, with a large clothes basket full of prizes, sat in a square pew below and handed out a prize to each child who answered correctly.

On 1 March 1847 he was presented by the College to the Rectory of Ufford cum Bainton in Northamptonshire; and in the same year he married Ann Judith, eldest daughter of Mr Smith Wormald, of Barton Hall, Barton-on-Humber. Ufford Church was five miles from Stamford, nine from Peterborough, and otherwise had little connection with the world.

* * * *

The thirty-three years passed at Ufford were uneventful, but filled with quiet, hard work; one of the first things done being the restoration of Ufford Church, which was sadly needed. Not only the church but the chancel had been filled with high red pews of all shapes and sizes; the pulpit and reading desk were in one block, and a curious heavy screen and rood-loft separated the chancel from the body of the church. He reformed all this not indeed in modern High Church fashion, but so as to be simple, comfortable, and in good taste. The Rectory itself had recently been much enlarged and improved; but it had a large garden which Mr and Mrs Paley found a field, and left a beautiful lawn with fine trees. The parish was carefully attended to, cottage lectures and Bible classes were started, and Mr Paley went regularly on Sundays and also on week days to teach and catechise the children. At that time the schools were taught by a succession of elderly dames; and one, a Mrs Sopps, combined the function of monthly nurse with that of school mistress. She had a birch rod tied with blue ribbon, and used it vigorously in school and in church. The boys as well as the girls were made to knit, and the art of bowing and curtseying to their betters was an important part of her system.

Mr Paley was a staunch supporter of the British and Foreign Bible Society, and with deputations would visit the towns and villages to hold meetings, driving long distances and having many adventures. On one occasion when entering the chapel which, as they thought, had been prepared for their reception, Mr Paley and the deputation were delighted to find a large and very devout audience assembled. It was not until the lecturer proceeded to nail up a huge picture of a tattooed savage, with which he was about to illustrate his remarks on missionary work, that the head of the officiating minister appeared above the pulpit to ascertain the cause of this unseemly interruption to his 'interval for silent prayer'; and the two gentlemen discovering that they had been taken to the wrong building had to beat a hasty and somewhat ignominious retreat. On another occasion the old groom, having used his resting time too well was found harnessing the horse wrong end on in the shafts, and, being expostulated with, said 'some folks likes it one way and some folks likes it the other'.

Mr Paley took great interest in the new art of photography, and his fondness for electrical and chemical experiments, and his use of microscopes and other scientific instruments, brought life and freshness to the village as well as to the Rectory. Later on he became much interested in the Higher Education of Women, and he prepared one of his daughters, now Mrs Alfred Marshall, for the Higher Local Examination as soon as it began. He was the first father to bring a daughter to Newnham, in the early life of which he took a keen interest, and was throughout a warm friend of Miss Clough's.

*   *   *   *

While an undergraduate he came under the influence of the Evangelical movement, and his personal relations to Simeon gave a tone to the rest of his life. He cared little for the outward forms of religion, and had a horror of all tendencies towards laying stress on these rather than on the spirit of religion. He made little boundary line between the Established Church and others: and he sometimes followed Simeon's example of preaching in Scotch Presbyterian churches. But he was in his way a loyal son of the Church. He published a small pamphlet entitled *Seven principal points on which all Christians are agreed*; and he collected from many sources a book of hymns 'full of the spirit and sweetness of our liturgy'. He arranged them in the order of the Collects which, 'like noble columns, have been introduced into Christ's Church at different times'. One who had frequent opportunity of hearing him preach describes his sermons as 'stately and ably expressed discourses, almost invariably marked by great polish, and which irresistibly reminded the hearer of some of the prominent Divines of the seventeenth and eighteenth centuries. In common with these they were at times marked by a quaintness in choice of text or treatment of subject such as we find equally in Laud and in his Puritan opponents. To see and hear the fine old man with his powerful face, white hair, and black gown—earnest, stately, and dignified—was like a leaf out of the history of the past, doubtless practically an anachronism, but none the less interesting and impressive.'

Printed in the United States
By Bookmasters